1

Taiji-Qigong in 22 Steps

Hartmut von Czapski

Photographed by Ellen von Czapski
and Hartmut von Czapski

Taiji-Qigong in 22 Steps

Hartmut von Czapski

Impressum

Bibliographic information of the German National Library:

The German National Library lists this publication in the Deutsche Nationalbibliografie; Detailed bibliographic data are available on the Internet at http://dnb.dnb.de.

© 2019 Hartmut von Czapski

Production and publishing: BoD – Books on Demand, Norderstedt

ISBN:9783752820072

Table of Contents

Foreword..11-13

About the person.......................................14-15

Qi Gong...16-18

Important energy centers..........................19-20

Energy intake and delivery points............21-22

The breathing...23

Basic stand..24-25

1) Initial step and breathing adjustment.................26-27

2) Open the chest.......................................28-29

3) Dance with the rainbow........................30-33

4) Part the clouds with swinging arms...................34-35

5) Rolling back of the upper arm..............36-38

6) Rowing in the middle of the lake.........39-40

7) Hold a ball in front of your shoulder....................41

8) Look for the moon..42

9) Turn hip and push palms.......................43-45

10) Riding posture with hand movement in the clouds..46-49

11) Fish out of the sea and look up to the sky........50-52

12) Qi regulation during upward and downward movement...53-55

13) Driving waves..56-59

14) Appease the chest and abdomen with qi...........60-62

15) Flying dove spreads its wings............................63-65

16) Two dragons loop around the pillar..................66-67

17) Let a ball jump open..68-69

18) Flying wild goose...70-71

19) The rotating flywheel...72-74

20) Raise your fist to attack.....................................75-77

21) Hold the sparrow's tail from left and right......78-84

22) Ending...85-86

Preface

These exercises are based on the theories and exercise series of Dr. Zhang Guilan (18 Taiji Qi Gong positions), Prof. Li Ding, Bambang Sutomo (28 Taiji Qi Gong positions) and Dr. Jiang Hao-Quan (the 8 basic Tai Chi positions).

The exercise series can be divided into 2 sections. Exercise 1-10 and 11-21. Exercise 1-3 should always be practiced together. Exercise 22 is the final exercise "opening and closing". It should be practiced at the end of each exercise session.

The most difficult exercises (10 and 21) I put at the end of each section. It takes a long time of practice to be carried out harmoniously fluently and yet correctly. Depending on your needs, you can also choose individual exercises in your daily program. The exercises that are hardest to do should be practiced to remove blockages. With all Qi Gong exercises one should consider his physical limits and slowly expand. As a beginner, it is advisable to practice body movements first and then add breathing. Breathing moves the energy in the body.

Qi Gong without correct breathing is called "empty Qi Gong". It is then nothing more than gymnastics. The internal energy control usually takes longer to practice.

When moving your hands, you should concentrate on the Laogong points in the palms.

The effects of Taiji Qigong are diverse: (Example exercises in brackets)

The increased oxygen uptake and increased blood flow affects all cells of the body, especially the brain and thus the memory. (9, 10, 15)

The sleep is better, but the daily energy is increased (basic level, 10, 14)

Deep breathing has a positive effect on the heart and lungs. The ECG is improved. (2, 4, 7, 8, 11, 15, 18, 19, 20)

The immune system is strengthened. (5, 11, 18)

The function of the digestive organs is promoted. (6, 11, 12, 13, 14, 15)

The autonomic nervous system is balanced, the mind calms down (basic status, 1, 6, 10, 11, 12, 13, 14, 18, 20, 21)Diseases of the reproductive organs are prevented. (21)

All joints and the spine become more supple and flexible. (3, 4, 6, 7, 8, 9, 11, 16, 21, 18, 19)

13

About the author

Hartmut von Czapski
Non-medical practitioner(Heilpraktiker) since 1984. Since 1987 exercise of acupuncture (Teacher Fr.Dr. Li Te, Chief Physician Nankei Clinic). Several stays in China with professional trainings.
1987 Scientific training of Uni.Tübingen passed: "Ecology and its biological basis".
Since1990 seminars, yoga and Qi Gong courses at various institutes. Since 1990 more than 1000 Qi Gong classes have been held.
Qi Gong Teacher 49009 des Mi Gong Rulai Buddhist Center for Qi Gong, Shanghai.
Training to Qi Gong Therapeut by Prof. Wu, Shanghai.
Lectures at the Medica in Dusseldorf on the treatment of incontinence with T.C.M .
1999 acupuncture specialist training for dentists; Teacher activity on various therapies.

Teaching Qi Gong Forms:

Medical Qi Gong according to Prof.Wu. Taiji Qigong after Li Ding.

Ten meditations on the mountain Wudang.

The Eighteenfold Method of Exercise.

The "Movements of the 5 Animals".

Qi Gong after Guo Lin for immune boosting.

The "Eight elegant exercises. "

"Wai dan gung"

Tai Chi for beginners by Dr. med. Jiang Hao-quan.

And much more.

Qi Gong

The term "Qi Gong" includes various types of exercises to absorb the "Qi", the life energy, and let it flow in the energy channels, the so-called "meridians". It is a substance that you normally do not see and grope, but can feel. The ancient Chinese philosophers thought that Qi is a source substance that originated in the Big Bang.

According to the Chinese view, Qi is a continuously moving and active substance, the basic substance from which the body originates. Qi receives the human life functions. By definition Qi in Qi Gong is an "essence" substance in the body with a certain energy. Qi can be formed, developed, transformed and moved in the body. Breathing moves the energy in the meridians. But even after a long practice of Qi Gong, one can move and absorb qi with the mind in the body.

These body and breathing exercises have at least a 4000-year-old tradition in China, as can be seen in descriptions of funerary offerings. There are many different types of exercises. On the one hand the soft Qi Gong, which contains many meditative elements based on the imagination and is often performed while sitting or lying down. On the other hand, we know the hard Qi Gong, which also strengthens the muscles and tendons and massages the internal organs.

Think e.g. to the achievements of the Shaolin monks in Kung Fu or to the acrobatic skills of the actors of Peking Opera. But Qigong exercises not only strengthen the body, but also calm the mind and regulate the autonomic nervous system.

A special form is the therapeutic qigong, which prescribes certain exercises for certain illnesses. Like any empirical science, qigong is always being developed. For example, in recent decades, e.g. certain new exercises against cancer are famous for their good results (Qi Gong after Guo Lin for improving the immune system). The high blood pressure research institute Shanghai has already published in 1978 works with reports on changes that causes Qigong on the ECG and EEG. Work has also been published that our sympathetic nervous system, which is active through prolonged stress, achieves relaxation through Qi Gong by predominance of the parasympathetic nervous system.In China, in many hospitals, in addition to the Department of Medicine, there is a Department of Traditional Chinese Medicine. This includes the treatment room for the Qi Gong therapist. Here the patient is not only taught exercises that he should practice regularly at home, the therapist also supplies the patient with energy that he himself has absorbed. Training to become a Qi Gong therapist is usually tedious. After 5 years of practice, you can teach Qi Gong exercises and also treat after 10 years. Mr. von Czapski has been trained by Prof.Wu as a Qi Gong therapist.

Important energy centers

Hui Yen, KG1. In the middle of the perineum, between the anus and the genital organ.

"Real" Dantian. It lies between the navel and the spine.

Lower Dantian, about 2 fingers wide under the navel. Approximately at the acupuncture point "Qi Hai", sea of energy.

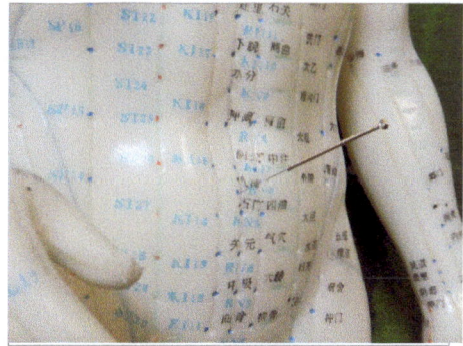

Middle Dantian, heart center. At the level of a hollow on the sternum, slightly below the nipples. Tan Zhong (KG17).

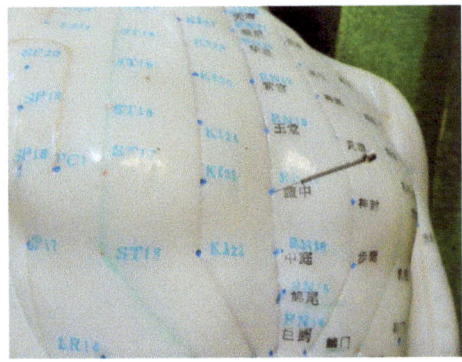

Upper Dantian, Yintang. Between the eyebrows, just above the base of the nose.

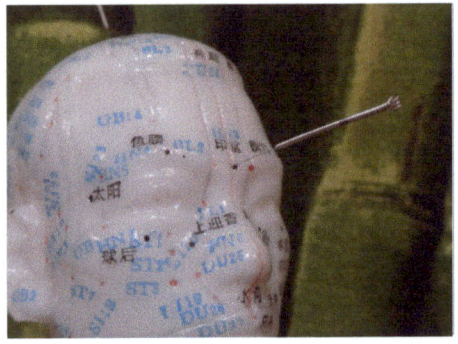

Energy intake and delivery points

<u>Yongchuan</u>. When we "dig our toes into the ground", a hollow is created below the base toe joints.
Point kidney 1.

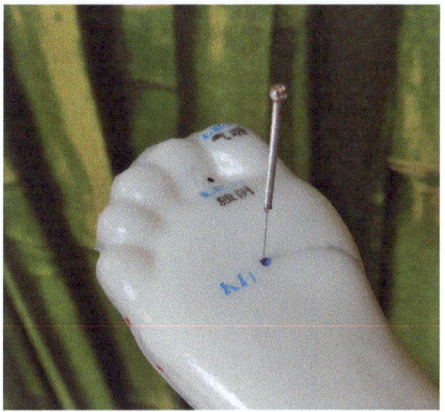

<u>Laogong.</u> If we bend the tip of the ring finger into the palm of our hand, we come to this point.

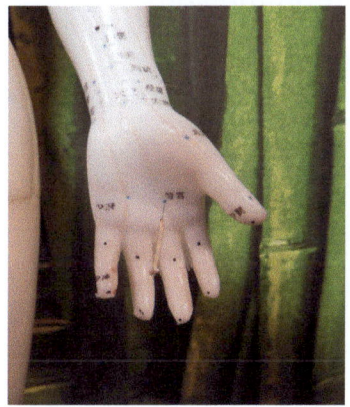

<u>Bai Hui</u>. Located in the middle of an imaginary line between the tips of the ears in a small hollow.

<u>Mingmen.</u> If you put the top of your index finger under the back of your costal arch and stretch your thumb towards your spine, you can use your thumb tips to reach the Mingmen point on the spine..

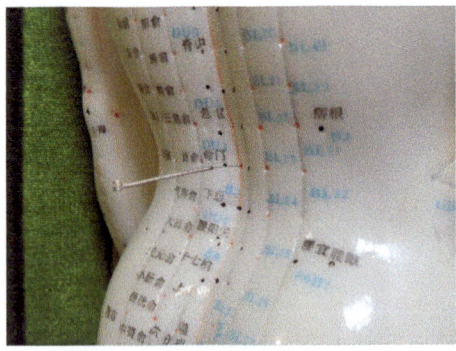

Breathing

Breathing should flow calmly and regularly, deep but relaxed and harmonious. Inhale through the nose, exhale through the mouth. Generally one can say: movement away from the body: exhale, movement towards the body: inhale. Movement up: inhale, movement down: exhale.

Basic stand

Stand feet shoulder-width apart and parallel.

Bend your knees slightly, but not beyond the tips of your feet.

Tilt the pelvis forward and down so that the lumbar spine straightens. For people with a hollow back, this is often difficult at the beginning, the upper body leans back. This should be straightened out.

The spine should be as straight as possible.

The chin is lowered slightly, the cervical spine is stretched.

All nerve impulses can flow more freely.

Take your shoulders back, then let your arms hang loosely. Relax your shoulders. Move your elbows slightly to the side. This creates some space in the armpits.

The hands are not stretched, loose, but slightly stretched in the palms to absorb energy. Slight, involuntary movements of the fingers are a good sign when consuming energy.

We can imagine that the feet, like the roots of a tree, reach deep. The upper body is movable like the branches of a tree without giving up the basic position described above.

Try to calm down, to absorb nature and the life energy in it. In addition, the inner state of mind should be like an empty white room.
The basic state should be taken for 1-2 minutes before and possibly between exercises to feel the effect.

Taiji-Qigong

1) Initial step and breathing adjustment

Place feet shoulder-width apart, parallel to each other.
Tilt the pelvis forward. Loosen knees.
Inhale , stretch your knees and raise your arms in front
of your chest to the level of your heart. Palms down. As
you exhale, lower your knees slightly and lower your
arms to the level of your lower abdomen.
Calm, slow, deep breathing.

2) Open the chest

Place feet shoulder-width apart, parallel to each other.
Tilt the pelvis forward. Loosen knees.
Inhale, stretch your knees and raise your arms in front of your chest to the level of your heart. Palms facing each other.
Point your palms towards your chest and exhale.
Put your hands to the side, stretch out the back, widen your chest and take a deep breath.
Exhale, hands stretched forward and down.
Repeat movement 8 times.

29

3) Dancing with the rainbow

Place feet shoulder-width apart, parallel to each other. Tilt the pelvis forward. Loosen knees.

Inhale, stretch your knees and raise your arms in front of your chest to the level of your heart. Palms facing each other.

Exhale, stretch your arms to shoulder height, palms up. Point your head up.

Straighten your head. Turn your left foot on tiptoe 30 ° to the left. Sit on tiptoe. Simultaneously turn your hips in the same direction. The weight is on the right side. On the right, the toes remain pointing forward.

Raise your right hand until Laogong is about 15 cm above Bai Hui.

With this movement we breathe in until the hand reaches the top of the bow, with the downward movement towards Bai Hui we breathe out.

Now change of sides. The right hand is stretched to the right at shoulder height. Palm up. At the same time move your left hand up over Bai Hui. Inhale and exhale during this movement.

Change the main leg to the left. The left foot is turned forward again. Turn your right foot on tiptoe approx. 30 ° to the right. Turn your hips to the right.

8 x each side.

33

4) Cut the clouds with swinging arms

Extend your right and left arms at shoulder height. Palms up. Breathe in.

Arms swing down. Palms towards the body. Exhale. Bend knees, back straight.

Cross your wrists, right arm up. Lift your arms crossed and inhale. Almost stretch your knees.

Spread your arms to the right and left and move them downwards, breathing out. Bend your knees. Cross your wrists, right arm up. Lift your arms crossed and inhale. Almost stretch your knees.

35

5) Roll back the upper arm

From the exhaled position of the last exercise, straighten up and turn your right arm backwards to the right. Inhale. Move your hips to the right. The left arm is stretched forward. Both arms outstretched at shoulder height.

When exhaling, move the back right hand past the ear and forward in front of the upper body so that the palm is facing down. At the same time hold the front, left hand in a bowl shape in front of the lower abdomen so that the upper and lower hand hold an imaginary ball. At the same time the hip turns straight forward again.

When inhaling, turn your hips in the other direction. Extend your lower hand back, your upper hand forward. Exhale, see above

6) Rowing in the middle of the lake

Hold both loose fists in front of both shoulders. As if we were holding two oars. Inhale this.

As you exhale, bend your knees and open your hands as if we were reaching for something beside of the knees.

Keep your back straight.

When inhaling, straighten up again, loosely close your fists and hold them in front of your shoulders, put on your elbows.

7) Hold a ball in front of your shoulder

When inhaling turn to the left, hold the right hand cups in front of the left shoulder as if we were holding a ball in front of the shoulder. The left hand hangs loosely. The right foot is turned forward on tiptoe. The right knee is pushed through. An oblique line forms from the right heel to the left shoulder tip.

When exhaling, turn back to the starting position. Let your arms hang loosely.

8) Look at the moon

The leg and body movement is the same as in the last exercise.

However, the arms are stretched upwards with the inhalation, as if we held the moon between our hands. The thumbs are spread apart. The whole body is stretched.

Exhale and turn back to the starting position. Let your arms loose. 4 x each side.

9) Turn your hips and slide your palms

Place feet shoulder-width apart, parallel to each other. Tilt the pelvis forward. Loosen knees.

Place your fists on your thumbs, with the inside of your fists facing up, on the pelvic bones.

When inhaling, turn the pelvis to the left, push your right fist forward; up to half of the possible stretching movement.

When exhaling, turn and slide the inside of your fist forward while opening your hand.

During inhalation make the previous movement backwards; up to half of the possible stretching movement.

When exhaling, put your fist back on the pelvic bones.

When inhaling, turn the pelvis to the right, extend your left fist as above.

When pushing the fist forward, the upper arm and upper body should form a right angle. Don't turn your shoulders forward and your back should stay straight.

It depends on the inner strength, not on the outer. Concentrate on Laogong. 4 x each side.

44

10) Riding posture with hand movement in the clouds

Place your feet a little wider than shoulder width, parallel to each other. Tilt the pelvis forward. Loosen knees.

The right hand moves in front of the face, the fingertips at eye level, about a hand's length from the face. Don't lift your elbows too high. The eyes follow the fingertips.

The left hand slides along the lower abdomen to the right side.

The weight shifts to the right, bent leg, the hip turns a little to the right. Inhale during this movement.

Turn the right, upper hand to the side of the shoulder and press the palm down. Breathe out.

The left hand simultaneously moves up in front of the face, fingertips at eye level.

The right hand pushes past the lower abdomen. The left hand moves past the face, next to the left shoulder. The hip turns slightly to the left, the weight shifts to the left leg. Inhale there. In this exercise, breathe only through your nose. At least 4 times on each side, or as long as it feels good.

This exercise should flow harmoniously, from right to left and left to right. It takes a long time for most students to achieve this.

Regulates the autonomic nervous system, has a positive influence on breathing and blood pressure. The hips are massaged.

For the beginner, it is advisable to practice these 10 forms before turning to the following. The first 3 should always be practiced together, the others can also be practiced individually or in a different order. Finally, exercise 22 "opening and closing" should be carried out.

48

11) Fish out of the sea and look up to the sky

From the basic stand, put your left foot one foot forward. The heel of the left foot is level with the toe of the right foot. The feet are shoulder-width apart.

We move our hands forward downward, in front of the left knee and put our wrists on top of each other. Breathe out.

Lift the crossed arms up and shift the weight onto the rear leg. The eyes follow the hands upwards. Inhale there.

The arms separate from each other above the head and move laterally in an arc downwards in front of the left knee, combined with the weight shifting forward. Breathe out.

7 x.

With one exhalation, put your left foot back and with one inhalation, put your right foot forward. Repeat the exercise on the right.

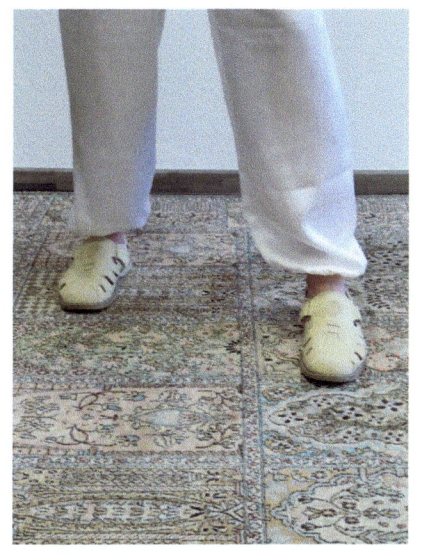

12) Qi regulation for upward and downward movement

Basic stand. Guide the loose, right hand up in the left axillary line. Inhale there. The left hand hangs loosely.

Turn your palm up at shoulder level and keep moving your hand over your head. Turn your hand there again and bring it down in front of the front midline of the body. Palm facing the body. Breathe out. The Qi follows the hand. Focus on Laogong. When exhaling, the inner qi follows the lowering of the hand.

This exercise has a very calming effect on the nervous system and blood pressure. Can be helpful for menopausal symptoms. It also calms the gastrointestinal system.

13) Drive waves forward

Basic stand, then put left foot shoulder width forward. Only put on the heel. The weight is on the right angled leg. The upper body leans back slightly, the arms are bent, loose fists are held in front of the chest.

Inside of the fist facing forward. Inhale there.

As you exhale, shift your weight forward to your left foot, which is now fully resting, and press your open hands down to the right and left of your left knee (the small wave).

When inhaling, move both hands forward and up. Shift weight strongly forward, then shift backward. Put the weight on the far right, only the heel on the left.

The big wave comes towards us and flows down the body.

Both hands press down on the front of the body.

Accompanied by exhalation.

Form loose fists and pull them in front of your upper body. Inhale there. See above.

4 x the small and large wave, then change of sides. Put your right foot forward and perform the same movements as described above.

14) The chest and abdomen soothed with qi.

Bend your right elbow outwards. Bring the loose right hand up to the right of the body. Inhale there.

Over the shoulder, the palm turns towards the face.

The head turns slightly to the left.

Exhale as the hand moves down.

The hand runs a short distance across the face to the breastbone and turns downwards at stomach level. The head turns forward again. Press your hand down in the center line and finally relax to the side. During the downward movement, also relax internally from top to bottom. At least 4 times on the right, then perform the same number with the left hand.

Has a very calming effect, also on the abdominal organs.

15) Flying dove spreads its wings

From the basic stand, put your left foot one foot forward. The heel of the left foot is level with the toe of the right foot. The feet are shoulder-width apart.

Shift weight back onto your right foot, bend your upper body slightly back. Inhale and spread both arms.

Palms forward.

As you exhale, shift your weight forward to your left foot.

Bring both hands forward like two wings.

When inhaling, shift the weight back. All fingertips (feathers) move towards the heart.

The fingertips run out over the chest, the arms spread out at shoulder height. The wings unfold accompanied by inhalation. See above...

At least 4 times, then put the other foot forward and carry out the exercise in the same way.

64

16) Two dragons loop around the pillar

Form two loose fists. The right hand hits the left chest, the left fist hits the right kidney lightly with the back. Inhale and stretch your knees.

As you exhale, bend your knees a little deeper. Both hands loosen, changing positions.

As we breathe in, we stretch our knees out more. The right fist hits the left kidney lightly with the back. The left hand hits the right side of the chest lightly.

Downward and upward movement with a straight back. Slight sideways turns only.

67

17) Let a ball bounce

While raising the left hand, the right knee rises to the right angle. Inhale. Exhale when lowering your hand and knee.

Then lift and inhale the right hand and left knee.

Exhale when lowering your hand and knee.

Change left and right several times.

Body coordination is promoted. Knee and hip problems are prevented.

18) Flying Wild Goose

Place both feet side by side, lift both hands sideways like the wings of a wild goose, almost merging the back of the hand above the head. Place on your toes and inhale deeply.

Exhale when lowering your hands and feet. Lower the knees slightly.

71

19) The rotating flywheel

Let both arms hang forward, take swing to the left, then swing to the right top, over the head to the left side.

Inhale during the upward movement. Exhale during the downward movement.

Swing down a bit to the right, then back up left, over the head to the bottom right. Get swing to the left, then swing back up to the right.

So do not perform a circular movement, but swing alternately to the right and left.

73

74

20) Raising your fist to attack

Take a basic position. Put both fists on the pelvic bones. Inside upwards. Each arm movement can be divided into 4 steps.

Inhale and push the fist with the inside up to half of the arm stretch, forward.

Exhale, turn your fist and push forward with the inside of the fist.

Do not twist the torso. The arm is stretched forward at shoulder height. It is not the external force, but the inner force that is decisive. Focus on the Laogong points.

Inhale and take back your fist.

Turn your fist about halfway through the stretch and exhale and lay on the pelvic bone. The inside of the fist points upwards again.

As you take one fist back, you push ahead with the other and perform the same movement on the other side. In harmonious change.

21) Grab the cock of the sparrow from left and right

Shift weight to the right, angled leg. Place your left foot on the tip of your toes next to your right foot.

Hands hold an imaginary ball. The right hand at the top, the left at the bottom at Dantian height. Inhale

Take a step to the left, put weight to the left, extend the left hand to the left at the same time. The left hand with the palm facing the face. We look at the tip of the middle finger. The right hand swipe down and right. The thumb stays on the belt line. Exhale.

Turn the left hand down. The right hand picks up the left hand. It's like holding a little ball. Both hands lead to the Dantian. Inhale. Weight to the right.

The right hand is extended to the right. The eyes follow the hand movement, the hip turns to the right. The left hand stops in front of the Dantian.

Press the right hand to the left at eye level. Exhale.

Shift the weight to the left. The hip turns slightly to the left. When the hand almost passes the face, raise the left hand at eye level. The right hand presses the left hand to the left without touching it.

Push both hands back up to the left at face height. Exhale and shift the weight to the left.

Move the right hand in wide arc up, right and bottom. Shift weight to the right. Reset the left foot next to the right foot. Inhale.

Hold a ball in front of the Dantian. The right hand down, the left up. Put weight to the left, right foot on the tip of the toes.

See above. Take a step to the right and spread out to the right and exhale...

It's not an easy exercise. Beginners should first practice the sequence of movements, later perform the correct breathing.

Generally one can say: hand movement away from the body: exhale, towards the body: inhale.

83

84

22) Open and close

At the end you should spread your arms 3 times to the side and breathe in; when exhaling, bring your hands to your chest.

We point our palms down, press our hands down in front of our bodies, bend our knees slightly. Keep your back straight. Breathe out. With a scoop movement we turn the palms up and raise our hands to the heart, inhaling as we do so.

Repeat this movement 3 times.

Also from the same author:

Qi Gong sitting

ISBN 9783750431409

This book describes 34 Qi Gong exercises performed while sitting. From simple movement exercises to Tuina massage exercises, breathing exercises and concentration exercises. These exercises improve the energy intake, strengthen the self-healing powers and balance the autonomic nervous system. They promote the ability to concentrate and inner peace. They have a positive effect on the digestive system, the muscles, the tendons, joints and the spine. The increased oxygen intake strengthens the heart and lungs.

It is very well suited as a exercise book for occupational medicine, for old people's home, as a com pletion for any Qi Gong course or just for in between for all office or computer workers. The many photos and the clear description make it easy to understand the exercises.

Available soon:

Qi Gong standing exercises

This book describes 23 Qi Gong standing exercises.

These exercises improve energy intake, strengthen the self-healing powers and balance the vegetative nervous system. You promote the ability to concentrate and inner peace. They strengthen the muscles and tendons. The standing positions of the 5 animals (monkey, deer, bear, tiger, crane) are also suitable for children.

Medical Qi Gong after Prof. Wu

In this book exercises are shown which, among other things in the following symptoms show excellent effects: high and low blood pressure, stomach and intestinal complaints, lung problems, insomnia, nervousness, lack of concentration, lack of energy, back pain and excessive stress.

With regular and persevering practice of Qi Gong, the practitioner can improve his health and find inner peace and relaxation. Since the exercises can be performed with varying degrees of force, they are also suitable for older, weakened people.